I0412734

THE STIMULUS PACKAGE

THE STIMULUS PACKAGE

WHY MEN CHEAT

Sheila Whalum

Copyright © 2011 by Sheila Whalum.

Library of Congress Control Number:		2011905397
ISBN:	Hardcover	978-1-4628-5185-0
	Softcover	978-1-4628-5184-3
	Ebook	978-1-4628-5186-7

All rights reserved. No part of this book may be reproduced or transmitted in any form or by any means, electronic or mechanical, including photocopying, recording, or by any information storage and retrieval system, without permission in writing from the copyright owner.

This book was printed in the United States of America.

To order additional copies of this book, contact:
Xlibris Corporation
1-888-795-4274
www.Xlibris.com
Orders@Xlibris.com
97288

CONTENTS

*

Introduction

*

Chapters

*

A Word to the Wives

SHEILA WHALUM

S heila Whalum is the wife of Dr. Kenneth T. Whalum Jr., Pastor of *The New Olivet Baptist Church,* Memphis City Schools Board of Commissioners and Author of *Hip-Hop Is Not Our Enemy.* They will celebrate 29 years of Marriage on June 19, 2011. Sheila is the mother of three talented sons: Saxophonist, Kenneth T. Whalum III (Crystal), Vocalist, Kortland Kirk Whalum and Trombonist, Kameron Timothy Whalum. She is President of Aliehs, Inc., (O'Sheilas Beauty and Barber Shop and Christ-Like Modeling). She retired from City of Memphis Government as the Deputy Director of Finance in 2010. In addition, she is the First Lady of The New Olivet Baptist Church located at 3084 Southern Avenue in Memphis, Tennessee.

Sheila is a graduate of Leadership Memphis. She has a Master of Business Administration from the University of Phoenix; a Bachelor of Arts Degree in Communications with a minor in English from the University of Memphis. She received a certificate from Rhodes College for the Institute for Executive Leadership. And, she was a product of Memphis City Schools where she was "Miss Carver of 1978."

She is past liaison for the City of Memphis for the Memphis/Shelby County Airport Authority Board. She served as committee member for the City of Memphis Hardship Deferred Compensation Plan; the Retirement System Investment Committee and the Operating Cash Committee. She is past board member for "Friends for Life Aids Awareness Program."

Her Professional accomplishments include:

> Certificate of Achievement (Program of Continuing Education in Public Finance) from Public Financial Management in Philadelphia, Pennsylvania. Certificate of Achievement from the State of Tennessee Educational Swap Training Course, Certificate of Completion for Arbitrage Compliance. Member of Government Finance Officers Association, United Way Coordinator for the Finance Division. Notary Public At Large, Family Medical Leave (FMLA) Coordinator for Finance. She is an At-Large Board Member for the Girl Scouts/Heart of the South, Co-Founder of BAMM (Bust-A-Move-Monday) for small businesses and is deeply involved in her church-The New Olivet Baptist Church—www.olivetbc.com

> *sheilawhalum@comcast.net*

ACKNOWLEDGMENTS

To the Man who treats me like a Queen:
Dr. Kenneth T. Whalum Jr.

To my talented three sons:
Kenneth T. Whalum III,
Kortland Kirk Whalum
Kameron Timothy Whalum

To my beautiful daughter-in-law, Crystal (Kenneth)

In memory of my mother,
Margaret White Lee

In memory of Dr. Loretta Bobo Mosley

In honor of my mother-in-law,
Mary Helen Whalum Rogers (Ormer)

To my Dad, Willie Peter Lee (Dr. Mel Seymore)

To my siblings: Kenneth, Angela, Wanda & Margaret

To the White, Lee & Whalum family

To The New Olivet Baptist Church Family

INTRODUCTION

The number of divorces in 2010 compelled me to write my third book, *The Stimulus Package: Why Men Cheat*. My other books are: *Destined to Be a Preacher's Wife*, and *Pretty Woman Too! The Truth About Jealousy Among Girls And Women*.

I almost gave up on writing this book on November 18, 2010, because every time I thought I was close to finishing this book, another couple would call it quits or bite the marital dust, if you will.

Even today, March 29, 2011, the day before I submit my book to the publisher, there is an article in the Wall Street Journal about Barry Bonds, a former Major League Baseball outfielder who cheated with another woman while being married. It was being reported just about everywhere: radio, television, internet, that various men were found to be cheating on their spouses by engaging in sexual acts, or they were on the verge of cheating. Not that this is a new revelation, of course!

I actually felt a little sad when I heard that the most beautiful couple, Tony Parker and Eva Longoria was divorcing. Eva had just received the "Freedom Award" in Memphis, Tennessee the day before the breaking news announcing her husband's infidelity.

I started taking the subject of cheating very seriously, especially among married couples, because I knew that it was not supposed to be this way, though it happens more often than not.

I want to begin with the original Playboy himself, Hugh Hefner. He is founder and *Chief Creative Officer* of *Playboy Enterprises*. He did an interview in August of 2010, and one of his statements was ***"wouldn't all men like to go to the Playboy Mansion?"***

I have a question for men? Have you ever wanted to be a guest of Hugh Hefner's at his Playboy Mansion?

History seems to suggest that some men apparently want more than one woman in their lives at a time, other than their wives.

That's kind of a no-brainer, but when you are operating under the Christian banner you are supposed to be held to higher standards in the spiritual realm than the natural realm. Christians are to be guided by their rule book: the Holy Bible.

Before I delve into *The Stimulus Package/Why Men Cheat*, I need to introduce some definitional clarity for several terms. I am sure you have heard about President Barack Obama's Stimulus Package. Please read the following information on it.

PRESIDENT OBAMA'S STIMULUS PACKAGE

When President Barack Obama took office in January 2009, the economy was stuck in the worst recession since the Great Depression, and America's financial system was on the verge of financial ruin. The depth of the recession in 2009 suggested that America needed a **stimulus** of about $1.2 to $1.5 trillion. The plan was to jumpstart economic growth, and save between 900 thousand to 2.3 million jobs.

In an effort to do that, the American Recovery and Reinvestment Act—the "Stimulus Package" was passed by Congress in February 2009. At a cost of $787 billion, the "stimulus" offered a package of tax cuts and new government spending that was supposed to kick-start economic growth.

The stimulus package allocated funds as follows:

1. $288 billion in tax cuts.
2. $224 billion in extended unemployment benefits, education and health care.
3. $275 billion for job creation using federal contracts, grants and loans.

Although the stimulus package was to be spent over ten years, the bulk of it was budgeted for the first three fiscal years: $185 billion in 2009, $400 billion in 2010 and $135 billion in 2011. The Plan did better than that. By October 30, 2009, over $241.9 billion had been spent: $92.8 billion in tax relief, $86.5 billion in unemployment and other benefits and $62.6 billion in job creation grants.

By October 8, 2010, the program had spent $554.4 billion: $243.4 billion in tax relief, $163.2 billion in entitlements and $147.8 billion in contracts, grants or loans. (Source: *Recovery.gov*)

As previously mentioned, the stimulus package was supposed to save 900 thousand to 2.3 million jobs. As of October 30, 2009, it had saved 640,329 jobs.(About.com).

Hopefully, you now have some understanding of what President Obama's stimulus package was about; now let's see what my stimulus package is about.

Contextual Definitions:

1. **Stimulus**—An action or condition that elicits or accelerates a physiological or psychological activity or response.
2. **Package**—A man's penis
3. **Men**—Married Men
4. **Cheat**—To engage in a sexual relationship outside of marriage.

As you can see, President Obama's meaning of "Stimulus Package" is totally different from mine.

The Stimulus Package: Why Men Cheat gives the number one reason why men cheat on their wives.

CHAPTER 1

My Experience

As a teenager growing up, I noticed that men were always very nice to me. I was around thirteen years old when I first began to notice how they would look at me. At that age I suppose you love the attention, not really knowing what it means. But you know when you've gotten "his" attention.

More often than not these were married men, whether at church or school, who would say things to me, or somehow "hint" at my best features.

I actually started liking the attention, and most of it came from church because that is where I spent most of my time. But what did I know at that age about men? The answer is, absolutely nothing!

Therefore, I went with the flow. Whatever attention they wanted to give me, I took it. I started developing physically more and more, and, naturally, "more" attention came. I am talking about attention from married men, mind you. Attention toward a thirteen year old girl.

In Junior High School, I received attention from married men. One even told me that when I got older; he was going to marry me. I believed him.

I found myself at many places that I should not have been. Men would buy me lunch. Men would buy me gifts. Men would take me shopping, all just to be with me: a pretty young thing, or as Michael Jackson used to sing, a "PYT".

I got my first job at a local department store when I was sixteen years old. Can you believe that at the age of sixteen, I was selling the best quality diamond jewelry in the City of Memphis? Was it because a white married man who was a high ranking manager liked me?

After I left that particular jewelry store and went to work at another jewelry store, another married man started in with the same attention. I must admit, he really got *my* attention. Things started getting too much for me to handle, so I left the company and went elsewhere. But he would not leave me alone. He would come to my new job and bring me gifts. He too said he wanted to marry me.

Guess what? At that new place of employment, the third jewelry location where I worked, another married man who was a manager harassed me until I had to file charges against him.

Though I was the young girl who had grown to be a young woman, I always had boyfriends close to my own age, but also, I had these married men at every turn waiting to do any and everything for me. I actually thought that was how it was supposed to be, married men with women on the side.

I am sure that if God had not intervened in my life at the age of twenty, I would not be where I am today, married for twenty—nine years to a Baptist Preacher. Sometimes I can't believe it myself. Me, a preacher's wife!

I met Kenneth at my church one Sunday evening in June of 1980. I was twenty, and he was almost twenty-four. He was in his last year of Law School at Temple University in Philadelphia, Pennsylvania.

His Father, who was the Pastor of Olivet Baptist Church, was our evening speaker that particular Sunday.

Kenneth took one look at me in the choir stand and made it his mission to get my attention. The rest is, as they say, history. After that Sunday, my life was never ever the same.

Kenneth was like no other man I had ever met. He was single, and smart, and brilliant, and witty, and good looking, and—most of all—he was a Christian.

I knew that God sent him to me, because God saw what path I was on. God knew that if I had stayed on that path I would not have gotten to know the joy of the LORD and all that it represents, and I would not have enjoyed such a wonderful and blessed life with my husband. Oh, by the way, we were destined to be together because Kenneth had seen a picture of me two years earlier when I was eighteen years old.

He worked at a men's clothing store when he would come home from school in the summer. He saw my picture on the wall at the store one day, because I had been a "living ad" for the owner of the store. He told the owner that he was going to meet me one day and he did. Not only did he meet me, he married me.

Kenneth and I created C.A.N.A. (Couples Achieving Newness Again), twelve years ago. This is a married couples' class that meets every Sunday at 9:30am for one hour at the New Olivet Baptist Church. We created the class because we have a great marriage, and we saw so many marriages that were in distress, and knew that is was not how God wanted marriages to be. We wanted to show that no matter what happens you can get your marriage back on the right track.

Looking back at my own past, and then looking at society today and seeing so many broken marriages, my husband and I decided to do something about it.

In my book, The Stimulus Package: Why Men Cheat, I want to show or attempt to show just why men cheat when they are married, and I want to show that it doesn't have to be that way.

CHAPTER 2

The Cheaters You Know

Tiger, Mark, John, Kelsey, Jesse & Eliot

It took me a little longer than expected to finish writing this book because it appeared that everyday married men were being caught cheating on their wives, and I would have to add another name to my Cheater's List.

I decided to highlight those that were in the news practically every day for a while. They are: Tiger Woods, Mark Sanford Jr., John Edwards, Kelsey Grammer, Jesse James and Eliot Spitzer.

I want to ask a question to those husbands: **WHY?** They had/have very beautiful wives who helped them to fulfill their dreams. These were very smart and intelligent women who were actually the strength of the family. Was it not enough for these husbands?

Why Tiger Why?

Tiger Woods confessed to his wife Elin Nordegren
that he cheated

Tiger Woods was born on December 30, 1975. He is an American professional golfer whose achievements rank him as one of the most successful golfers of all time.

Formerly the World No. 1 golfer, at the time of his divorce he was the highest-paid professional athlete in the world.

Tiger Woods and Elin Nordegren were married on October 5, 2004. They were married for approximately five years. On December 11, 2009, Woods announced he would take an indefinite leave from professional golf to focus on his marriage after he admitted infidelity with *many* women.

Elin was featured on the cover of People magazine September 6, 2010. In the article she is quoted as saying, "What I want people to know is how hard it's been. It's hard to think you have this life, and then all of a sudden—was it a lie?" She says, "I believe any crisis in life makes you more mature and look at life slightly differently. I know I have some healing to do, but I am excited to start the next chapter of my life." Tiger and Elin officially divorced on August 23, 2010.

Why Mark Why?

Mark Sanford Jr., was born on May 28, 1960. He is an American politician from South Carolina, who started serving as that state's governor on January 15, 2003. A member of the Republican Party, he served from 1995 to 2001 as Congressman in the United States House of Representatives for South Carolina's 1st congressional district, where he held conservative positions. In 2002, he was elected the 115th Governor of South Carolina and re-elected in 2006. Governor Mark Sanford left office on January 12, 2011, a position he held for eight years, after a scandal surrounding his infidelity.

Mark Sanford Jr. and Jennifer "Jenny" Sullivan were married on November 4, 1989. They were married for approximately twenty-one years. On June 24, 2009, Sanford resigned as chairman of the Republican Governors Association after he publicly revealed that he had an affair. A Charleston, South Carolina judge ruled that Governor Mark Sanford's admitted affair with an Argentine woman was grounds for his wife, Jenny, to divorce him.

Jenny Sanford requested a divorce from Governor Mark Sanford on the grounds of his adultery. The divorce was granted, and Sanford became the first sitting governor to divorce in the state of South Carolina.

The divorce was final on March 19, 2010, after Jenny Sanford testified in family court in Charleston that her husband referred to his mistress as his "soul mate" and requested time and time again to be permitted to see her.

In Jenny's book, *Staying True*, she states, "I see now that June 24, 2009, was a day that changed forever the trajectory of my life, but it did not change me."

Why John Why?

John Edwards was born on June 10, 1953. He is an American politician, who served as a U.S. Senator from North Carolina. He was the Democratic nominee for Vice President in 2004, and again in 2008.

John Edwards and Elizabeth Anania were married on July 30, 1977. They were married for approximately 33 years.

On August 7, 2008, Edwards admitted to ABC News correspondent Bob Woodruff that he had an affair. On January 21, 2010, Edwards issued a statement admitting that he fathered a child with his mistress. Edwards' wife, Elizabeth separated from him and intended to file for divorce. She died on December 7, 2010 of cancer.

John Edwards' wife Elizabeth tells a heartbreaking story in her book *Resilience*, of how her husband of thirty-three years cheated on her. Yet she denies in that book that the little baby he held in a hotel room with his mistress is her husband's baby. She states that the mistress approached her husband first. Elizabeth states that he made a mistake. Duh! Later, she re-writes that it is her husband's baby.

Why Kelsey Why?

Kelsey Grammer was born on February 21, 1955. He is an American actor and comedian. He is best known for his two-decade portrayal of psychiatrist Dr. Frasier Crane in the NBC sitcoms *Cheers* and *Frasier*.

Kelsey Grammer and Camille Donatacci married in August 1996. They were married for approximately thirteen years. Camille filed for divorce in June 2010, but it was not final until February, 2011.

Camille's, now ex-husband, **Kelsey Grammer**, dumped her earlier this year to be with a twenty-nine year old flight Attendant. He and Kayte Walsh married on February 25, 2011.

Why Jesse Why?

Jesse James was born on April 19, 1969. Jesse was star of the television show, "Monster Garage", shown on the Discovery Channel from 2002-2006. He had a love for motorcycles and opened his own motorcycle shop—West Coast Choppers—in Long Beach, California in 1992. He built custom bikes for megastars.

Jesse James and Sandra Bullock married July 16, 2005. They had been married for approximately five years when it was reported that James had an affair with a tattoo model and with other women as well. James did not address the charges directly, but made a public apology for the "grief" he had caused his wife.

Sandra divorced her husband Jesse James on June 28, 2010, after a string of his infidelities.

Why Eliot Why?

Eliot Spitzer was born June 10, 1959. He is an American lawyer, former politician of the Democratic Party and currently a political commentator. He is currently the co-host of *Parker Spitzer*, a talk-show on the CNN cable network. He served as the 54th Governor of New York from January 2007 until his resignation on March 17, 2008 in the wake of his involvement as a client in a high-priced prostitution ring.

Eliot Spitzer and Silda Wall were married on October 17, 1987. They have been married for approximately twenty-four years as of this writing on January 10, 2011, and are still married.

The next few chapters will take you through a typical marriage cycle to give you a better understanding of how marriages typically start, and then how they often end when men (husbands) cheat. The chapters following attempt to show that even when infidelity occurs, the marriage doesn't have to end with divorce. It can end in redemption.

CHAPTER 3

What is Love?

"What is love?" is one of the most difficult questions facing mankind. Love is a strong and positive emotion of regard and affection.

Love is patient. Love is kind. Love does not envy. Love does not boast, is not proud, and is not rude, or self-seeking.

Love is supposed to be there when you need it. The late vocalist Donnie Hathaway said, "Where is the love you said was mine oh mine 'til the end of time? Where is the love? Marriage is supposed to be about love. That is what the wives of those previously mentioned famous cheaters thought.

Marriage is not easy. Just like you plan for so many things in life, you must plan for your life in marriage.

Couples often plan for the wedding, which is for one day, but do not plan for the marriage which should be for a lifetime. I have heard so many wives asking that question from Donnie's song, "Where is the love you said was mine, oh mine until the end of time?"

I have found through life and through research that most things in life come in threes, and marriage is no different. You should plan for your marriage to have a beginning, middle, and end. Those are the three stages of marriage.

The problem that many couples often face is that they don't know what stage they are in, and so they don't know how to handle a particular situation when it develops.

If you are married, did you know that your marriage really isn't about you? It is about God being glorified! It is about God the Father, God the

Son, and God the Holy Spirit being exalted. As you move further into this book, you will see what I am talking about.

God created marriage. Remember Adam and Eve? The Genesis account says, *Then the Lord God made a woman from the rib he had taken out of the man and brought her to the man. Then Adam said, "This is now bone of my bones and flesh of my flesh; she shall be called woman for she was taken out of man," For this reason a man will leave his father and mother and be united to his wife and they will become one flesh. (Genesis 2:18-25)*

In the New Testament, in the Book of Ephesians, it says, *So ought men to love their wives as their own bodies. He that loves his wife loves himself.* It goes on to say, *For no man ever yet hated his own flesh, but nourishes and cherishes it, even as the Lord nourishes and cherishes the church. For we are members of his body, of his flesh, and of his bones. For this cause shall a man leave his father and mother, and shall be joined unto his wife, and they two shall be one flesh.* (Ephesians 5:28-29:31)

The Old and the New Testament are saying the same thing. So what happened? What went wrong? Why isn't married life giving you . . . LIFE? Husbands, why did you have to go and cheat?

To better understand possibly what went wrong, let's look again at the Three Stages of Marriage as noted by Dr. and Mrs. Lynwood Davis of the Torch Leader Daily News: The Davises call them the three stages of marriage:

1. Endearment
2. Adjustment
3. Commitment

The first stage is **Endearment**. This stage is very easy and very short—lived. It is untested. It is really Fantasy Land because all you think about is each other, romance, and sex. This stage may last 4 or 5 years. It varies depending upon the circumstances. Adam and Eve went through the Endearment stage. They had a perfect relationship with each other. If you don't believe me, read it for yourself in the book of Genesis. It was perfect, and they were perfect. But, as *perfect as everything was, they did* not stay in this endearment stage. Simply defined, the word endearment means, the outward expression, verbally and physically, of affection. According to Dr. and Mrs. Lynwood Davis, whom after my research, I believe gave the best answer: a couple cannot establish their marriage here in this stage.

The second stage is ***Adjustment***. And the adjustment stage is the most difficult stage of the three. The word adjustment simply means to make light changes to make something fit or function better. It means to adapt to a new environment or condition. In this stage, you have been married for a while and both of you realize things have changed. The adjustment stage is where you will find all of your problems.

His fault, her fault, the children, the finances, the job, school, you name it. The Davises, who have a dynamic ministry on marriage, state all marriages enter this stage, but few ever leave it. That means they do not deal with their real problems, and they often end up miserable, become cheaters, or end up in divorce court, which is tragic when you consider that with a little work those couples could have gotten to stage three!

Adam and Eve were forced to accept the fact that they could not live outside of Paradise the same way they did inside Paradise. What did Adam and Eve do? They adjusted to each other's needs.

If you want to keep and save your marriage, you must realize that it is not whose fault it is, but where do we go from here? You must adjust to whatever the situation is that you cannot change. Or, as so well stated by the Davises, "Fight the problem and not each other"!

You have probably heard of the story of Cain and Abel. Adam and Eve had two sons. They lost their son, Abel because his brother Cain killed him in a fit of jealous rage. But even after that terrible ordeal, Adam and Eve REFUSED to let it interfere with their relationship as Husband and Wife. They stayed together, and they continued to "be fruitful and multiply" as they had been instructed and empowered to do by their Creator.

The lesson is that if there is a major problem or issue, then the two of you must push to get out of the adjustment stage, and into the third and final stage: ***Commitment***. The sad thing is that per the Davises, very few marriages ever reach this stage. That is why the divorce rate is so high.

It is often reported that the divorce rate in the United States is fifty percent. Americans for Divorce Reform estimates that forty to fifty percent of marriages will end if current trends continue. Divorce rates only tend to go down primarily because more couples live together without marrying, which is not—I repeat—NOT the Christian way.

In the Commitment stage, both of you have gotten the adjustments right. You have adjusted your marriage to deal with moods (PMS or menopause for both) and mid-life crisis for him.

You have adjusted your marriage to the different situations and different circumstances that are sure to come. It means you ENJOY each other's company, and you have included God back into your marriage.

Earlier in the chapter, I mentioned the 'two of you", but there really should be three persons involved in a marriage. That's right; every marital relationship should be a menage' a trois, with **God**, **husband**, and **wife** as the participating parties! In the book of Ephesians it says, *for we are members of his body, of his flesh, and of his bones* (5:30). So many couples are leaving God out of the equation at each of the three stages.

God has not changed. His word is still the same. God is waiting to give you as a couple something new, like he did for Adam and Eve, if you will commit your marriage to Him.

When Adam and Eve got to this last stage after all that had happened, God gave them another son named Seth because they held on, persevered, and committed to each other. They loved each other, and they believed in His promises. You can too!

CHAPTER 4

Fun~The Beginning

L et the fun begin! Let's go back. You have just gotten married and the both of you have pledged to live happily ever-after. Life is so wonderful! Don't you remember when you said it—"I Do!" Oh, and "With this Ring, I thee Wed." Both of you put on your wedding bands. But, then something happened along the way: the wedding band disappeared from the husband!

It has been brought to my attention by the Holy Spirit that a lot of married men are *not* wearing their wedding bands these days. My first reaction was, so what! No Big deal! As long as my husband wears his wedding band, what do I care? But, it went deeper than that. I do care! I care because it means something, and that is why I chose to write about it.

As I mentioned, my husband and I created CANA, Couples Achieving Newness Again, a married couples' class at The *New* Olivet Baptist Church in Memphis, Tennessee where he is Pastor.

We surveyed the class and realized that a lot of the married men in the class were not wearing their wedding bands. My husband decided to issue a challenge to those men to honor their wives and wear their wedding bands, and they accepted.

We then went beyond the classroom and surveyed the congregation and found the same thing—the absence of the wedding band. Again, he challenged them and now most, if not all, married men of The New Olivet Baptist Church are wearing their wedding bands.

We then said to each other, what is that about? Why do so many married men not wear their wedding bands? We tried to get to the root of the problem, so, we continued our quest for the answer. This is what we got:

> "My wedding band is too small" (married for 10 years). "I
> don't like jewelry". "I forgot to put it on" (for the past 5 years), or
> "It will get caught in the machine at work" (but it is Sunday).

I then decided to survey the professional, corporate world in which I work. To my surprise, I saw the exact same thing: Doctors, Lawyers, Bankers, Professional men, all married, but no wedding band. Sure, they loved their wives, and they have even mentioned them a few times, but no wedding band. I wanted to come right out and ask each of them, "Why don't you wear your wedding band?" But I figured that I already knew the answer. I can give many reasons why men don't wear their wedding bands, that is why I wrote *The Stimulus Package, Why Men Cheat.*

I even saw the "Oprah Show" recently where her friend Gayle stated that she had gone on a date with a particular man. The evening was progressing very nicely until he mentioned that he was married. She stated to Oprah that she was somewhat hurt and then asked the question, "Why didn't he wear his wedding band? If he had, I would have known that he was unavailable when I first met him."

To top it off, I was in the presence of a marriage counselor who was giving a major presentation to thousands of people about marriage. To my surprise, the marriage counselor who was married did not have his wedding band on. I thought, God, what is this? Something is definitely wrong with this picture. I am almost certain that when a man and a woman get married, it is stated somewhere in the vows, "With this ring (meaning wedding band), I thee wed!" I did mention this earlier.

In addition to me knowing the real reason why some married men do not wear their wedding bands, another reason is that it is just *not* the "thing" to do in this day and age, they say.

However, the vows that you took with your wife concerning the wedding band could now mean that you no longer honor her with that simple act of not wearing it. It is not supposed to be this way.

God had me to expose this evil. Husbands, this is a trick of the enemy! This is even considered spiritual warfare. Have you ever thought about how it makes your wife feel on the inside when you don't wear your wedding band? Husbands, what if she didn't wear hers?

If we are to have the holy marriages that God is calling Christians to have, then the wedding band must become visible. I honor and respect all married men who wear their wedding bands. You show that you love, value and cherish the relationship with your wife; with the one that you will spend the rest of your life with.

Okay, let's get back to the topic at hand: Fun. In the beginning, marriage was a lot of fun. It just could not be any better. You are really getting to know each other. He can do no wrong and she can do no wrong. It is like Heaven. You only have eyes for each other. You hold hands, you touch each other all over, you kiss all of the time and you make love quite often. ☺

The fun continues. You start talking about your life together and when you might have children together; you may even talk about the house you will buy; the new job after you get that college degree; that Master's Degree or better yet that Doctorate. The dreams are endless.

You tell each other that if you have to, you will struggle through life together with **love** because love is in the midst. Every day you wake up, you can't wait to start another day with the one you love, BUT . . .

CHAPTER 5

Familiarity

After several years—five, seven, nine years, a shift happens; you feel a change. You begin to be very familiar with the one you love.

You are used to the same routine. Yes, you now have that new house, that new job, that new baby or two, and so what's the big deal. Now someone is bored, but it isn't the wife, because she has plenty to keep her busy. The husband now feels he has accomplished his duties as a husband. So why not start having some "real" fun like he used to.

"My wife won't notice a thing", he tells himself. "She is too busy taking care of the children, cooking, washing clothes, maybe even in school herself. She knows me", he says. "She is familiar with me. What harm can I do if I want to now start looking around with my eyes? What is wrong if I branch out a little and have lunch with my co-worker who happens to be a female? She knows I am married. I don't wear my wedding band all the time, but she knows. After all, I am innocent. I love my wife." BUT . . .

CHAPTER 6

Life Happens

It is ten years later, and you realize that life just keeps on happening. Not only are you familiar with your wife, your children, and your way of doing things; but now you spend most of your time on everything but having fun with your wife.

You start staying at work later or you go play golf or have drinks with your co-workers, and all the while life passes you by. You are feeling more secure and self-confident, probably because of the good home your wife has made for you, and the sense of order that is provided in that home, so you decide it is time to branch out. You start getting more into yourself, fretting about how you look to the opposite sex. You update your wardrobe depending on your finances.

You now want to be back on the scene, but this time without your wife. Somewhere in the back of your mind, you really don't see anything wrong with the steps you are about to take. You are innocent! You are just going to hang out with the fellows at the bar, at the gym. You may even have a regular schedule of going to see your mother. But, the point is life is passing you by because you feel you are stuck in the house helping your wife with the children or with her *honey-do* list.

You now have confidence in your ability to be a husband. You don't need your wife as much in public so you will go solo on many occasions.

CHAPTER 7

Things Change

Attention Wife: Something is not right. You feel it. He feels it. Something is not clicking. When did the laughter stop? No more smiles. The house is feeling empty. You are feeling empty and he appears to be adjusting to this change just fine.

He has the car to leave and go to work. You are stuck at home without a car. By the way, you don't drive. You don't have a job. Your heart starts to sink. You become suspicious because you are locked in mentally and physically.

Or, you have a job. You have a car, but you know in your heart that things are not like they used to be, and it is getting worse. What do you do I have been asked many times?

Well, first things first. Whether you have a job or not, I believe that every wife should get up every morning, preparing to go somewhere though she may never leave the house. This will trigger success in every wife's effort to keep her power. You must do something.

After speaking with so many wives, about why they think their husbands changed, they all had their many different reasons and a lot of them blamed themselves.

CHAPTER 8

Fun Goes Out The Door

Like the reigning King of the Blues and recording artist for over four decades, B.B. King says, *"The Thrill is Gone"*, and like the late American R&B and soul singer/songwriter, and record producer Luther Vandross said, "A house is not a home when there is no one living there." The question is, How did the two of you get to this? How did it get to fussing and cussing every day? How did it get to the two of you faking the funk? Pretending to be lovers when you are not.

Why did you let the fun go out the door? You are the leader of the family. You're the head of the house. Did the wife do something? Did she nag too much because you would not help her around the house? You wouldn't help her with the children? Did she not cook enough for you? Did she gain too much weight? Did she not wear negligees every night for you? Just what did she do? You never told her. You just started having fun outside of the house. The fun in your marriage left. She loved you in the beginning, and she loves you now, but your love is now elsewhere. What happened to the Fun?

Well, let me just say that men are going to have fun by any means necessary. There was an article in The Wall Street Journal in 2010 entitled, "Only in Japan: Real Men Go to a Hotel with Virtual Girlfriends." The article states that in Atami, Japan, once a popular honeymoon resort town, the population is shrinking due to lower marriage rates.

However, they have created a dating simulation game where the men are real and the girls are cartoon characters on a screen. The man can choose one of three females named goodie Manaka, sassy Rinko or big sister type Nene—to be a steady girlfriend. (See below):

The man taps a stylus on the DS touch screen in order to walk hand in hand with his virtual girlfriend all offered for a fee by Love-Plus, a product of Konami Corporation played on Nintendo Co.'s DS videogame system. (WSJ by Daisuke Wakabayashi 9/1/10).

As I mentioned, men will have fun by any means necessary. What happened is that the focus of "attention" got lost. Communication stopped. Your top priority was no longer your wife.

As you can see by now, the pattern started. So often it starts with the absence of the wedding band, but not always the case. Marriage is fun if you keep the main thing the main thing-your wife.

Trust me. I understand that the wife has a responsibility to maintain as well. I am all about the wife being the girlfriend that you met. She must keep up if she is to stay in the game of marriage.

CHAPTER 9

Eyes Roam

Mr. Big Stuff, who do you think you are, Mr. Big Stuff? "**Mr. Big Stuff**" is a **song** by R&B singer Jean Knight that was released in 1971. Does anyone remember it?

Well, according to Rachel, her husband John, started acting like Mr. Big Stuff. She asked John, "Why have I noticed that your eyes now roam somewhere else and they are not on me.

When I mentioned it to you before, you said that I was seeing things; that I was imagining things. You even said that I was crazy, but guess what? That is a lie. I saw you John!

I saw you look at the Polka dot dress. I saw you look at the girl with the big butt (I have one too!). I saw you look at the woman who was showing all her breast. I saw you look at the teenager with her short-shorts.

I remember every instance because each time you did it, you took a part of my heart. That stare, that look, made me think that I was no longer enough for you. You could not separate me from the children and being the wife and all that it represented, so you started looking outside the home. You wanted to be Mr. Big Stuff.

You wanted more attention from other women than you did from your own wife. You would frequent the malls and even if you had your wedding band on, you would hide your hand in your pocket.

John, I never said anything. What was that about? I did not feel that it would lead to a divorce, but, I felt it would lead to something. Don't you remember, former President Bill Clinton with Monica Lewinsky. Don't you remember former New York governor Eliot Spitzer? Don't you care that you are about to cross the line?

What is it that makes men cross that line? Sure, men will look at other women. They have eyes, but when those eyes go into lust, and the wife can see it, then she knows that her husband has just crossed the line.

Wives, as I mentioned, you must stay in the game. You have to be what he looks at, and many of you are. However, if he is being cool, and stylish, why are you outdated? Why are you looking like the Grandmother? Stay where he is, on the same level. If his eyes roam to something that you can handle, then handle your business.

You see, a man likes what he sees. So how are you looking? I read an article where a man said that the "stock market" is like a beautiful woman; always fascinating. In other words, possessing the power to charm or allure; it means captivating. She is of great interest or attraction; she is enchanting and charming. He goes on to say she is mystifying. She has the ability to confuse or puzzle someone mentally.

Investors invest in stocks. Husbands invest in Wives, and Wives invest in Husbands. The Stock Market can be called a Bear Market where the prices of securities fall or it can be a Bull Market where the securities are rising. Wives, how is your husband's investment looking?

CHAPTER 10

Crossed the Line

Well. You did it. You crossed the line. You cheated on your wife. You had an affair. You say it is not an affair, but it is/was. You even paid for sex. How dumb is that in this economy when you can get it for free!

There are countless men who crossed the line which I previously mentioned, such as Tiger Woods, Mark Sanford, John Edwards, Kelsy Grammer, Jesse James and Eliot Spitzer. Of course there are many others; not to mention those who may not have engaged in sex while married who I would call "on the verge cheaters", but they committed other unfaithful acts like Tony Parker.

Tony Parker was born on May 17, 1982. He was born in Bruges, Belgium, but raised in France. Parker is a professional basketball player with the NBA's San Antonio Spurs, where he plays point guard.

Tony Parker and Eva Longoria married July 7, 2007. They were married for approximately three years until Eva was blindsided by reports that Tony was unfaithful with a close friend of hers. Eva allegedly discovered that Tony had been exchanging personal texts with a mutual female friend for nearly a year. Tony reportedly admitted to his wrongdoing. On November 17, 2010, Longoria filed for divorce from Parker in Los Angeles, citing "irreconcilable differences".

Also, others that have allegedly been on the verge of cheating are former President Bill Clinton, former Mayor of Detroit, Kwame Kilpatrick, legendary basketball player, Michael Jordan, prolific NFL quarterback Bret Favre, and Academy Award Winning Actor Morgan Freeman.

In *The Commercial Appeal*, a local newspaper in Memphis, there was an article entitled "If husband won't rebuff flirty friend, do it yourself." This article is written by Marcy Sugar and Kathy Mitchell (11/23/10). The article basically says that a particular couple regularly goes camping with another couple. However the wife of the other couple lost her balance while they were all sitting in the sand. She put her hand on the man of the other couple and left it there for an hour. When the wife mentioned the behavior to her husband and stated she felt the woman was totally out of line, her husband responded, "you are overreacting."

This is typically how cheaters start out—downplaying the situation. When the wife calls the husband out, she is often told she is overreacting. But because she loves him, she ignores those incidents until often it is too late.

Grammy Award winning artist R. Kelly has a song called "When A Woman Loves, She Loves For Real." And he is correct. When Actress Linda Evans was on the Oprah Show in 2010, she stated how when she was twenty-eight years old, her husband left her for a fifteen year old named Bo Derek. She stated it broke her heart. She was indeed beautiful, but somehow that wasn't enough. She then stated she loved another man after the divorce (a younger man) and that she had a face lift just to try and keep him (that wasn't enough either.) Remember, R. Kelly said, "When a woman loves, she loves for real".

Linda Evans (the beautiful woman who played the character named Crystal in the television show, "Dynasty") was willing to do whatever it took for love, but apparently love wasn't enough either. Could it be that "passionate sex" is what is needed to fulfill a man?

CHAPTER 11

It's Over

Is the marriage really over or not? What would Jesus do if he were married? How many times would he forgive his spouse? How many times will you forgive yours?

Is it over in your heart? Oftentimes, it is not over for the husband, but it is for the wife. If the husband is bringing something of value to the table, the wife will stay with her husband for her children's sake or for her security sake, but deep down, she feels it is over.

She will then shut down emotionally, sexually, and otherwise and go through the motions. However, sometimes she meets that younger *renderoni* who puts that "spark" back into her being.

Husbands, think before you act. How many times will you keep making the same mistake? You could be held accountable for your wife's actions. The beautiful actress Elizabeth Taylor was married eight times. She went to the well eight times! I mean, she actually said "I do" eight times, sometimes more than once to the same man! I surmise that she valued the unity of marriage. Who wants a broken marriage? Apparently, she kept trying to get it right.

CHAPTER 12

Another Statistic

Why do you want to be a number added to the divorce data? Why would you want to be considered as just another cheater who was added to the statistical data of following after his flesh and not after God? Yes, it will take a lot of work to stay focused and faithful, but it can be done if you want to do it.

The late Pastor John Osteen, father of bestselling author and Pastor Joel Osteen, used to say, "How big is your want to?" You have got to want to keep your marriage in right standing with your wife and with God.

It hurts God when married men, who are supposed to be the leaders of their homes, tear it down by the mere act of selfishness on their part. They want to have their cake and eat it too.

When you become a cheater, you often have a double whammy against you, because not only are you a cheater statistic but oftentimes, a divorce statistic.

When you divorce, you are saying, 'I don't'. There was an article written in Newsweek on June 21, 2010 entitled, *I Don't: The Case Against Marriage*, by Jessica Bennett and Jesse Ellison. It states, "Some weddings are fun, but too often they're a formulaic, overpriced, fraught rite of passage, marking entry into an institution that sociologists describe as broken."

The article goes on to state, "once upon a time, marriage made sense. It was how women ensured their financial security, got the fathers of their children to stick around, and gained access to a host of legal rights. But forty years after the feminist movement established our rights in the workplace, a generation after the divorce rate peaked, and a decade after Sex and the City made singledom chic, marriage is—from a legal and practical standpoint, at least—no longer necessary."

I can accept their right to their opinion, but who has the final say-so on marriage? The answer is, the one who created marriage. In the United States in 2010, there was a video that went viral with over one million views.

It was called "Black Marriage Negotiations". According to an article in Ebony Magazine in January, 2011, the video deals with the fact that most singles want marriage and the safety, security and financial resources that come with sanctified coupling.

A Pew Research Center/Time Magazine study recently found that fifty-eight percent of never-married single Americans want to be married, as do the twenty-two percent of those who are divorced or widowed. (Ebony/ Adrienne Samuels Gibbs).

With that said, The *Stimulus Package* is right on time for you to change your course of action so that you will not become a cheater. Marriage is a good thing.

CHAPTER 13

Why Men Cheat

As you read the list of some of the reasons why men say they cheat, feel free to add your own because I have a feeling the list can get pretty long. I have also added what some wives have said.

I asked several men who were divorced, why did they cheat? This is what they said:

-The Power of a Woman
-They were somewhat "mothered" by the wife
-Peer Pressure from other men
-They needed Passionate Sex
-The wife had gained weight
-She didn't look like she looked 10 years ago
-She didn't respect me
-She cheated on me
-I need more than one woman in my life
-She didn't have excitement any more

The wives said they felt their husbands cheated because they can't help themselves. They cheat because of their ego. They are not disciplined. They cheat because of what they see. They cheat because as a man they need to always feel powerful and most men feel powerful in two ways: in the pockets and in the pants, oftentimes not at the same time. In other words, they cheat because of their "**stimulus package**".

The list will just continue to get longer and longer. Go ahead and add yours, but I believe the single, real and number one answer is found in this scripture, 3 John 2: *Beloved, I wish above all things that you would prosper and be in good health even as your soul prospers.* **Men cheat because their soul is not in good health. In the book of Proverbs, chapter 6, verse 32, it states, "But whoso commits adultery with a woman lacks understanding: He that does it destroys his own soul."** The soul comprises your thoughts, your will, and your emotions.

When men cheat, I believe they have stopped living the best life that was ordained for marriage. But, it is not too late to get another chance.

CHAPTER 14

Mission Impossible

In 1966, when I was 6 years old, there was a TV series called Mission Impossible. Mission Impossible had action, adventure and drama. The show was created by a man named Bruce Geller and lasted on TV for 7 years. It featured such fine men as Greg Morris, Peter Graves, Peter Lupus and Leonard Nimoy. They were a team that carried out highly sensitive missions.

They worked for a *Government agency* as spies and specialists who were given "impossible missions" and so, their job was to unmask criminals, rescue hostages or take care of whatever the assignment was for the day. They would use whatever means necessary to accomplish their mission though most of the jobs they encountered were impossible. They used technology like hidden cameras. They used drugs and even greed to achieve their goals.

But today, there is another story, the remix. This story does not have an ending date. It is called Mission "Him" Possible. It too has action, adventure and drama. The story of David and Bethsheba had major drama. David "lusted" after a beautiful married woman named Bethsheba when he saw her taking a bath from his rooftop.

While her husband, Uriah was away at war, David, being the King, was able to seduce her to the point where she became pregnant with his child.

He tried to come up with a scheme where as King, he had authority to have Bethsheba's husband Uriah come home to rest for awhile, but it backfired because her husband didn't want to come home. He was on a mission.

If he had come home, David was going to force Bethsheba to go to bed with her own husband so she could say she was pregnant by her husband. Since that did not happen, David had the husband killed . . . .It is a great story, so read 1ˢᵗ Samuel to get the rest of the story.

And so, this story—Mission Him Possible, just like Mission Impossible had and has impossible tasks to complete, but if you hang with God, you will see that the things which are impossible with men are possible with God. How do you think David got out of that mess if it wasn't for a Possible God?

If you need your marriage restored, it's possible with God. Whatever the situation calls for, it is possible with God.

Chapter 15

God's Plan

The Power of Love After You Have Had Broken Love

God's plan is for marriages to stay together and thrive through the good times and the bad times. And He wants you to pray together so that your prayers won't be hindered. The book of Ephesians says, *the husband ought to love his wife as himself.*

There have been many divorces over the years, and there will be many more. There are married couples on your jobs; couples in your families who have gone through and are going through a divorce right now. There are couples who are saying they are just not happy and they don't know why. Therefore, I want to offer a few suggestions before you say IT IS OVER!

You must understand that "Everything Must Change". That song has been recorded by such artists as Bernard Igner, Oleta Adams, Barbara Streisand and so many others. It says:

> Everything must change
> Nothing stays the same
> Everyone must change
> No one stays the same
>
> The young become the old
> And mysteries do unfold
> Cause that's the way of time
> Nothing and no one goes unchanged

There are not many things in life
You can be sure of
Except rain comes from the clouds
Sun lights up the sky
And hummingbirds do fly

Winter turns to spring
A wounded heart will heal
But never much too soon
Yes everything must change

You must allow change to be a part of your marriage. If you have been married, 5, 10, 20, 30, 40, or 50 years, somebody has changed, and it's not all bad, but you need to know how to accept the change.

You must adjust your marriage and realize that you are married for a common goal. Your individual goals changed; your spouse's individual goals changed, and to stay married your common goals must change.

Marriage is not easy. As I previously mentioned, a program on CBS reported on January 9, 2011 that marriage is at its lowest rate since the 1970's. Also, I mentioned that you plan for so many things in life, but you must also plan for your marriage. Many couples are letting a lot of things and people interfere with their marriage.

What about the reality shows of women, and of men? The cell phones, blackberries and e-mails, twitter, baby—mama drama and any other thing you can throw in. Is it interfering with your relationship with your wife? It is time now to get back to the basics, back to **love**. Corinthians 13:13 states, ***And now these three remain: faith, hope and love. But the greatest of these is love.***

God's plan is still *love*, and what the power of love can do for you. God is love! Should it be enough that God is love and should I have that same love?

But, you must know it is not that easy. Did you know that when your heart stops loving, all manner of things happen to you that are not good?

I asked in chapter two, what is love? Love is a feeling of a strong attachment. It is induced by that which delights or commands admiration, kindness or devotion to another. Love is intimate, Love is affectionate and love is tender.

As Christians, we should feel God loving us. We should feel him all over. He delights in us, he admires us, he is devoted to us, he is kind to us, but so often we get so wrapped up in another kind of love. The love that hurts; that strong emotion that takes our heart into a whole other dimension; A love that causes us to do wrong when we know better. A love so strong for him or her, or for things, that we wonder what does God have to do with this?

We say "This is my love and I can love any kind of way I want to." But that is foolish love. You see, if you keep your priorities in check with loving God first, he is going to give you everything you need, want and desire, and all of that comes in the form of a wife, a house, a car, a job, good finances, good family and good relationships.

But some of you have become counterfeit lovers to God. Your love of God is not real and it is evident by your action of cheating on your wife. Husbands, think of the pain you caused your wife when you broke her heart by breaking your vows to her. By the way, you made those vows to God and to your bride, and you made them in the presence of witnesses. If you haven't broken your vows through cheating, but you know you're perilously close to crossing that line, think of the pain you will cause her. Imagine what it would feel like if she cheated on you! Would you be able to take it? How would you react? Would you be nonchalant, or inconsolable? Would you be forgiving or vengeful? Would you want to hurt your wife, or the one she cheated with? Try to put yourself in her shoes.

Think back. Think back to the day you met her. Think back to the rush of lust when you first saw her body. Think back to the animal attraction that made every moment with her a pleasurable experience. Think back to your wedding day. Think back to how she looked as the church doors opened to reveal her standing there.

Think back to how nervous yet proud you were as she stepped softly on the rose petals that had been strewn in her path. Think back to how she almost floated on air! Think back to when the preacher said, "Who gives the bride to be married?" and you stepped over to take her hand.

Think back to that look in her eyes as she saw beyond your eyes into your soul, and poured love into your very mind. Think back to when you said, "With this ring, I thee wed, and with all my worldly goods, I thee endow." Think back to the prayer the preacher prayed over your marriage. Think back to her voice, and how it sounded like music when she said confidently, "I do." Think back to how you really meant it when you said the same. Think back to that kiss you thought would never come because the preacher was taking so long to finish the ceremony! Think back. Now, why do you want to hurt her? The answer is, you don't.

Whatever you have done in the past, it is not too late. In the last book of the Bible, Revelation, Jesus says, *And he that overcomes, and keep my works unto the end, to him will I give **power** over the nations.*

I have seen and heard of such great influence by those who possess perceived power. The sad irony however is that often; most of those with power don't have power over themselves. That is the power to live moral lives, the power to control the flesh, the power to love one another, the power to honor their wives by wearing their wedding bands.

It's time to rediscover your power: the power of love. I challenge you to find the right source. Get to know the one who creates the POWER. God will give you the specific ability to produce your own reality just because you loved . . . . .

You see, you must overcome that cheating spirit. You have not experienced the real love, which is God's love, until you overcome that cheating spirit.

*God so loved the World, that he gave his only begotten son—Jesus—that whosoever believeth on him shall not **perish**, but have everlasting LIFE.* Now that is a show of love.

Remember behind every great husband there is a great wife!

*

A Word to the Wives

*

CHAPTER 16

(It's Not Always His Fault)

One night while at home in bed, I was flipping the remote control going through the channels as we all do and the movie **"Gone with the Wind"** was on. For some reason, I decided to stay on that channel and watch this movie. It is a famous movie set in 1939. Some of you may remember it. The two main characters in the movie are Scarlett O'Hara played by Vivien Leigh and Rhett Butler played by Clark Gable.

It is a Love-Hate Love Story between the two. In addition, Scarlett has emotional problems and lastly, her love comes just a little too late. Scarlett and Rhett date for a while then they get married. They have a good life so it seems. They have it all: They have the looks: he is fine and she is pretty. They have a beautiful house, cars, money, you name it and they have it, but, Scarlett is in love with somebody else. There is a song by Jasmine Sullivan called " I am in love with someone else?" Scarlett is in love with a guy named Ashley Wilkes who is about to marry another woman named Melanie, who happens to be Scarlett's best friend.

Though Scarlett tells Ashley that she is in love with him he still chooses to marry Melanie who he says would make him a better wife.

Well, since he marries Ashley, Scarlett goes ahead and marries Rhett, though she didn't love him. Throughout the marriage, they fought like cats and dogs.

As time went on her husband Rhett continued to try and please her, but it wasn't enough. She still wants her best friend's husband.

When her friend Melanie becomes ill, She and her husband goes over to their house. Her friend dies and she tries to comfort her friend's husband, the man that she truly loves. She tells him that now that your wife has died we could be together, all the while her husband, Rhett was watching and listening.

But, the man she loves turns her down. When she realizes that he doesn't love her after all, she decides she needs to play her cards right. She looks around for her husband and realizes that he is gone. Rhett tips out when he sees how his wife is acting over this other man.

Rhett finally realizes that this woman, his wife whom he tries to love over and over again, doesn't love him.

When Scarlett finally makes it home, she sees that Rhett is packing and is about to be out. She then proceeds to tell him, "I really do love you and give me another chance and he realizing that he has done all that he can to get this woman to love him—he tells her, *Frankly, my dear, I don't give a Damn!" and walks out the door forever.*

You see Scarlett was **Gone with the Wind**—What do I mean by that?

While wind has many, many meanings, the one I chose to use means a current of air carrying an odor, scent or sound . . . Scarlett was blown and tossed by the wind. She was carrying a scent and it was not a sweet smelling scent though she wore the finest perfume. *She wanted a Married Man!* She also carried a sound that was painful to listen to.

Apparently, she did not know about the book of James in the Bible where it says:

> *²Consider it pure joy, my brothers, whenever you face trials of many kinds, ³because you know that the testing of your faith develops perseverance. ⁴Perseverance must finish its work so that you may be mature and complete, not lacking anything. ⁵If any of you lacks wisdom, he should ask God, who gives generously to all without finding fault, and it will be given to him. ⁶But when he asks, he must believe and not doubt, because he who doubts is like a wave of the sea, blown and tossed by the wind. ⁷That man should not think he will receive anything from the Lord; ⁸he is a double-minded man, unstable in all he does.*

It says, consider it pure joy when you face trials of many kinds, but not when you bring them upon yourselves. Scarlett knew that man was married and so was she.

The Book of James goes on to say, let perseverance finish its work so that you may be mature and complete—not lacking anything. In other words in spite of difficulties, obstacles, discouragement, keep trying to reach your goal, but Scarlett was in the wrong so she could never reach her goal.

Right after it says "Lacking anything," verse 5 gets specific. It says, "If any of you lack **Wisdom,** you should ask God, who gives generously to all without finding fault, and it will be given unto you."

What is Wisdom? It is the ability to discern or judge what is true, right, or lasting; It is insight into something.

Why, would James be specific here? It is because a lot of people think that their lives are their own and they can do what they want to do. Scarlett wanted to do it her way and it brought her heartache. She not only lost one man, but two men.

I remember when I almost didn't use WISDOM, and it would have changed the course of history for my life. When I met Kenneth T. Whalum, Jr., he wanted me. He wanted attention, affection and agreement, but I was dating another guy that I thought I couldn't live without. Everyone, but me could see that he was not the one for me, but I was in Love. No matter how nice Kenneth tried to be, and we had even met in church, I was **not** using God's wisdom. I remember even writing Kenneth a "Dear John Letter" telling him that he was the nicest guy, but that I was going to stay with the boyfriend I had, but guess what, for some reason I never mailed the letter to Kenneth while he was at Temple Law School in Philadelphia. I remember praying to God. **I said, "God, Kenneth will be coming home from Law school in May and what am I to do?"** I can't have these two boyfriends any longer since he will be moving back to Memphis. And because the scripture says, if you lack wisdom, you should ask God who gives generously to all without finding fault, and it will be given to you, I asked God for wisdom and the rest is history. We will celebrate 29 years of marriage on June 19, 2011—Yeah!

You see sometimes, we just don't know what is good for us, but if you are on God's side, he will show up just in the nick of time.

The scripture also says, but when you ask, you must believe and not doubt, because the one who doubts is like a wave of the sea, blown and tossed by the wind. Those who doubt should not think they should receive anything from the Lord; they are double-minded and unstable in all they do.

And so, as I expound more on "Gone with the Wind" this phrase means doubters—those who don't believe God's word. Those who don't study to show themselves approved. Those who are constantly blown and tossed by the wind. Those who are unstable in everything they do.

Just like Scarlett who ended up with a broken heart because she was double minded, God says those who doubt should not think they will receive anything from the Lord.

Scarlett could never get it together because her heart had been broken and never made whole.

You see until you ask God to fix your broken heart from whatever relationship that hurt you whether it was a husband, wife, sister, brother, aunt, friend, stepfather, or stepmother, and whether it was yesterday, last year or many years ago, only until you ask God to fix it and make it whole will it just continue to affect everything around you.

When a heart is healthy it loves everybody. When a heart is broken, it picks and chooses whom it wants to love. That's why you can treat this person mean and treat that person nice. That is why there are so many men cheaters (husbands).

You (Wives and Husbands) are not using **wisdom** to ask God to fix your broken heart so you go through life in "pieces" never quite getting where you want to be. In actuality, you are doubting God and what he can do for you and therefore you are tossed about as the wind going here and there. And as God looks as you trying to do life yourself, he says go ahead. Don't expect my blessings, you are double-minded. You have your own Wisdom.

He says, "If you had my wisdom, you would be **born again**. I have tried and tried to help you. I have given you so many opportunities and so much time, It is now 2011 and you still are playing me for a fool! You continue doing what you want.

"You really think you have time, but just when you think you have one more chance to get it right with me, I just might say to you, ***Frankly, my Dear, I don't give a damn—In the Biblical sense?***

CHAPTER 17

Worthy of Wisdom

Husbands, before you think this chapter is not for you, listen to this: I thought that I would be focusing on the good of a woman, but God turned it around where the Man comes out smelling like a rose and the woman—well . . . . keep reading. I realized that God was helping a brother out.

The 7th chapter of Proverbs *warns men to* stay away from women who don't have wisdom because these women can ruin a brother. This chapter in the Bible (NLT) is entitled—Warning Against the Adulterous Woman

¹ My son, keep my words
and store up my commands within you.
² Keep my commands and you will live;
guard my teachings as the apple of your eye.
³ Bind them on your fingers;
write them on the tablet of your heart.
⁴ Say to wisdom, "You are my sister,"
and to insight, "You are my relative."
⁵ They will keep you from the adulterous woman,
from the wayward woman with her seductive words.
⁶ At the window of my house
I looked down through the lattice.
⁷ I saw among the simple,
I noticed among the young men,
a youth who had no sense.

[8] He was going down the street near her corner,
    walking along in the direction of her house
      [9] at twilight, as the day was fading,
      as the dark of night set in.
    [10] Then out came a woman to meet him,
    dressed like a prostitute and with crafty intent.
      [11] (She is unruly and defiant,
      her feet never stay at home;
    [12] now in the street, now in the squares,
      at every corner she lurks.)
    [13] She took hold of him and kissed him
      and with a brazen face she said:
      [14] "Today I fulfilled my vows,
and I have food from my fellowship offering at home.
      [15] So I came out to meet you;
    I looked for you and have found you!
      [16] I have covered my bed
      with colored linens from Egypt.
      [17] I have perfumed my bed
      with myrrh, aloes and cinnamon.
[18] Come, let's drink deeply of love till morning;
      let's enjoy ourselves with love!
      [19] My husband is not at home;
      he has gone on a long journey.
    [20] He took his purse filled with money
    and will not be home till full moon."
    [21] With persuasive words she led him astray;
    she seduced him with her smooth talk.
      [22] All at once he followed her
    like an ox going to the slaughter,
    like a deer[a] stepping into a noose[b]
      [23] till an arrow pierces his liver,
    like a bird darting into a snare,
    little knowing it will cost him his life.
      [24] Now then, my sons, listen to me;
      pay attention to what I say.
    [25] Do not let your heart turn to her ways
      or stray into her paths.
[26] Many are the victims she has brought down;

her slain are a mighty throng.
²⁷ Her house is a highway to the grave,
leading down to the chambers of death.

God is telling the man—forget the woman, you better have wisdom, if you want to live. You can call wisdom Mary, Jane, Sue, Tanisha, but only an understanding of his word will keep you out of trouble.

I really didn't expect that so I said okay God, what can I tell the women? Are we really that bad? Women, we are worthy of wisdom, but oftentimes we use the wrong wisdom. Wisdom means knowledge, it means you have insight. You have good sense and you have a good attitude.

Think about what I just said: Knowledge. What do you know? Wisdom starts by learning the ABC's. When you are in pre-school or kindergarden, they start teaching you those sweet ABC's. This might seem elementary but let's try it—

ABCDEFG

HIJKLMNOP

QRSTUVWXY and Z.

Now I know my ABC's, next time want you sing with me.

So the alphabet is a beautiful thing, but women who don't have wisdom often misuse these alphabets. If they had wisdom, they would not do some of the things they do. Those same alphabets that we used to adore, women without wisdom somehow pushed them to the side and the *devil picked up* every letter and used them.

Let' start with "A".

The devil makes many women:
Angry—Look at their faces
Many women *Betray* their sisters and brothers.
They don't act like *Christians*. A lot of women who call themselves Christians are doing everything but being a Christian. Think of the women you know.
They act like the *Devil*. Look at what they do.

They act as an *Enemy* of God. They show this by how they act and live and how they show that church is often a nuisance to them by not coming because they have other things to do.

They behave just like a *Fool.* Aretha Franklin says –Chain, Chain, Chain, Chain a Fool. This person is out of control.

They *Grieve* the Holy Spirit. The Lord speaks in different ways to his children. They know when the Lord is speaking or nudging them but they don't have time.

They *Harm* others with their words. They curse people.

They have *Idol* Gods. They love material things. The list goes on and on . . .

Jealousy is in their eyes. Women are so jealous that they can't hid it. They *Kill* with their tongue. They talk about you and lie on you.

They *Lust* after so many things. They want everything they see.

They get *Mad* at the drop of a hat. Let somebody jump in front of them while they are driving. It is called road-rage. They are ready to run them off the road.

Women get *Naked* when they shouldn't, like when the eagle flies on Friday night and it's not with their spouse.

They *Object* to doing it God's way. They say I don't care what the Bible says, I will do what I want to do.

They *Perform* how they want in this life. They don't care about being excellent in all that they do. They perform at whatever pace they want to, often being very lazy in everything they do.

They are like a *Quake*—which is kayotic, just come in out of nowhere. Just out of order. If you are out of order, you are a Quake.

They *Rattle & Roll.* They are always making noise. Think about a dice game. You rattle the dice, then, you roll the dice just to see where it will land and on what number. Well, a lot of women are just like the dice. They don't know which way they are going, they are rattling, and once they start rattling, then they start rolling just any direction to see if it is happening over here or happing over there, never getting anywhere.

They *Shake.* They are always shaking something, even if it is their tail feather.

They *Trespass*-They don't care that it is your property, they want it and they are going to take it.

They are *Ungodly* based on their actions.

They are *Violent*. They are always looking for something or someone to tear down.

They are *Weak*. These women without wisdom are weak in the mind; weak in faith because they won't give God a chance.

They do *X-rated things*. Things mostly done late in the mid-night hour, and I don't mean praying.

A *Yoke is on* their life but they don't realize it. It is really around their neck *and* until they give their lives to God, others will yoke them around life.

They Zig-Zag in Life! They really don't know if they are coming or going. They start this project, don't finish it, then move to the next one. It is 20 years later and they are still Zig-Zagging in life. It is almost as if they are drunk. The sad part is that many of them have been in church all of their life, but they missed something. They didn't allow the holy spirit to come in and change them because they say they are in charge of their life and they got this . . . .

So, there you have it, the ABC's

A, B, C, D, E, F, G,

H I J K L M N O P

Q R S T U V

W X Y & Z

Now I know my abc's, next time won't you sing with me.

So you see, the alphabets started out good, but evil came in.

What I have found in the word of God, is that history repeats itself. There were many women in the Bible who had the same problems many of us face today.

There was a Queen named Athaliah She was the (Queen of Judah) back in 836BC. She was the daughter of *Israel's* King *Ahab* and of *Jezebel*. She didn't use wisdom. Jealousy was in her eyes. She saw threats coming her way to take over the throne, so she had people killed, but in return she was killed. Not having wisdom got her killed.

What about Queen Esther? She replaced Queen Vashti. She was a good person but got caught in a lie because of her step-father who told her to lie. She lied because Mordecai wanted her to be Queen so badly that she hid the fact that she was Jewish. She denied her birthright. Well, that was not wise.

Then there is Sarah. Sarah was the wife of Abraham. Because Sarah was childless, she appointed Hagar, her Egyptian servant to have a child with her husband Abraham. When Hagar conceived the child and named him Ishmael, Sarah got mad and put her out and had her own child. That was not wise to deny the son the right to his father.

Although, history shows us that there is nothing new under the sun, we must wander like Paul when he says in Galatians 5:17 "For the good that I will to do, I do not do; but the evil I will not to do, that I practice. This is where lack of wisdom comes in. It amounts to your flesh waring against your spirit.

Many of you today are not women of wisdom because you operate in the flesh (the outside) and not the spirit (the inside). What are you going to do about it? The choice is yours. Just know that God is giving you another chance today to get the right kind of wisdom. Repent of your ways and live the life he has called you to live . . . Ask for Godly wisdom. Ask for good sense. Ask for a good attitude, and you can be a woman worthy of wisdom.

The Bible goes on to say wisdom is better than rubies. That means that your big ruby ring with diamonds means nothing if you don't have wisdom? If God can tell man whom he created before woman that he needs wisdom more than a woman, please—what do you think God thinks about your ruby ring?

To get wisdom, be obedient to God's word. Read the Bible, come to church, and learn to live that holy life. That is a woman worthy of wisdom.

CHAPTER 18

Makeover

Everywhere you look these days, you hear about women getting a makeover. I am sure you have seen those reality shows where they are spending months away from their homes, leaving husbands and children behind. There have been shows such as **"Extreme Makeover"**, **The Swan** *and* **I Want a Famous Face.** Those who participated on these shows were not satisfied with some features about themselves so they went to extreme lengths to start over and hoped to feel good about themselves.

In most cases, when those people on television had gone through the process of a makeover, they either looked better or totally different than before. As I mentioned in Chapter 10, Linda Evans makeover came in the form of a facelift and it wasn't enough to keep the love of her life.

A few years ago, it was reported in our local newspaper that 70% of American women didn't like their bodies and they were spending anywhere from $3,000 to $150,000 to make a change.

Recently, The American Academy of Cosmetic Surgery reported growth in all areas of cosmetic procedures. Botox treatments were up 11% over the previous year meaning Botox for the belly and any other area of your body, breast augmentation was up 8.5% and liposuction remained the most popular surgical procedure. It stated that shows like "Extreme Makeover" only fueled that trend.

The problem is that so many women are fixing up the outside. They are constantly changing the outside appearance in some shape, form or fashion, all for the praise of someone else. But, before you can have any kind of makeover, it first starts in the attitude of your mind? Your mind is the element in your thought processes. It controls your feelings, your reasoning, your thoughts, your perceptions, your will, your memory and your imagination.

Wives, if you choose to have a makeover, please make sure it is what you want and it is for you. It should not be to please anyone else. It is very important to make sure your spirit, mind and body are in sync.

My company, Christ-Like Modeling teaches girls and women, to be the best for *themselves*: and to let the good that is on the inside show-up on the outside which is the Christ-Like Attitude.

It also teaches them the fine art of original style. Style is defined as a mode of fashion, as in dress, especially good or approved fashion; elegance; smartness. This is what I represent. People often see me and my husband meeting for lunch. We normally arrive in separate cars. I will step out of my two-seated Mercedes Benz, in my fitted jeans with my black fendi leather jacket looking fly and looking like his girlfriend. This scenario often starts a rumor that Pastor Whalum has a girlfriend. I love it! Wives, be your husband's girlfriend.

EPILOGUE

Painted with Praise

I will praise thee; for I am fearfully and wonderfully made: marvelous are thy works; and that my soul knows right well.

*David was talking here and we should all know how David messed up most of his life—But, each time, he knew God saw what he did. He knew he could not hid from God so he would just call out to him—**O'Lord, thou has searched me and known me.***

Painted with praise—what does that really mean? Are we to be overjoyed every day? Are we to be happy every day? Every time someone sees us, are we supposed to be beaming. Are we to be like the sunshine?

Even when things are *not* right in our lives; the marriage is not right; the money is not right; our career is not right, and it is so easy to complain about the ills of life. Are we really supposed to be happy? The answer really is YES.

We should know that praise is some kind of applause. We praise our children for doing something good. We praise someone for getting an education, a new job and so forth.

God says praise is to express gratitude for personal favors: in other words, you give approval to someone. You compliment someone. Husbands and Wives should be praising each other because praise is reciprocal: If I say you look nice, you would say back to me "so do you" You look nice too. Well that is what God does, if you praise him, he will praise you.

Praise is just like a beautiful garden, if you want to plant nice tomatoes, you put the SEED in the ground and water it and watch your nice tomatoes grow. If you want a beautiful marriage, plant the right seed. God is the same way. If you give to him, he will give to you. If you give him money, he will give money back to you. If you give him time, he will give time back to you.

When you are driving down the street and you see an accident and you were not in it, you praise him.

When you are in the line to use your debit card for grocery and someone in front of you has to use food stamps—praise him.

When you buy that expensive gas for your car and pass someone on the bus stop praise him.

When you praise him, you are saying to God—**marvelous are they works**. Isn't he marvelous today?

God is marvelous to me for so many reasons: My three talented sons, my retirement. 29 years of marriage and still going strong; and good health. Therefore I will praise him for he made me and I am fearfully and wonderfully made and marvelous are his works.

Now, you may think praise is all that, but when you add *painted with praise*, it is explosive because it means God is covering you. That is why you must be happy every day. Painted with praise means you are decorated. People know when you are coming because there is something special about you. They see you from afar off.

Think about a dull room. If you applied some beautiful yellow paint, wouldn't it come alive? If you paint a room red, see that it makes you want to eat, I did, and a light blue room calms you and helps you to relax. Think about this, the walls are praising the painters because they covered them and made them over and gave them a new look.

I will praise thee; for I am fearfully and wonderfully made: marvelous are thy works; and that my soul knows right well.

God is saying that he put me so together that I am in awe. I am scared of myself. Who would do such a creation of me?

God put each of you so together that he got all the pieces together, fitted them perfectly, then put your soul in there. He made you a praiser. He then praised you and since it's reciprocal, you should have praised him back.

Don't you realize that the first applause you ever got was from God. Sheila has arrived!

Believe God's report that you are wonderfully made.

Husbands, Wives, put down your sin nature. Put the past behind you. Step up to the plate and be a praiser with the right paint and then began to see the marvelous works of God in your MARRIAGE!

To order other "WHALUM" products, e-mail *sheilawhalum@comcast.net,*
or *go to www.olivetbc.com* or call 901-454-7777.

Pretty Woman Too!
The Truth About Jealousy

Saxophonist
Kenneth T. Whalum, III

Hip-Hop is not our Enemy
by Dr. Kenneth T. Whalum, Jr.
Kameron Whalum on book cover

America Bless
God- Vocalist
Kortland Whalum

Stone nyc
Jewelry
by
Crystal Whalum

Future Books
Why They Hate in Memphis
&
The Twelve Men in My life

www.ingramcontent.com/pod-product-compliance
Lightning Source LLC
Chambersburg PA
CBHW021246280526
45784CB00005B/2254